How Can I Help My Alcoholic Husband?

Cherry Parker

How Can I Help My Alcoholic Husband?

ISBN - 13 - 9781508799979
ISBN - 10 - 1508799970
Copyright © Cherry Parker 2013

www.cherryparker.co.nz

It is not the intention of the author to
provide any type of counseling in this book.
The opinions offered and thoughts conveyed
are those of the author. No responsibility or
liability can be accepted by the author for
any actions taken by any person
or organization.

Every truth passes through three stages
before it is recognized.
In the first it is ridiculed
In the second it is opposed
In the third, it is regarded as self evident.

- Arthur Schopenhauer

Please note:

The author is not a counselor, doctor, therapist, psychiatrist, life coach or health professional.
This book is my own personal opinion gleaned from living with an alcoholic partner, my husband.

For the purposes of this book the alcoholic will be referred to as "he".
If you fear for your own safety seek a safe refuge.

In an emergency the front of the phone book lists numbers for urgent help.

Seek professional people who are trained to assist you if necessary

Introduction

My first book was **"Living with an Alcoholic Husband - a true account of living with and without a husband addicted to alcohol."**
It is my personal account of living with a husband addicted to alcohol, on a roller coaster ride of hope and despair, love and loathing, embarrassment and anger, dreading each day. How I slowly came to realize that I always wanted him to change. I was wrong. It had to be me who changed.
I describe how I reached those conclusions, the choices I made and acted on to improve my life.
I wrote about my experiences in the hopes that either a partner or a drinker may be helped. If one person sees themselves reflected in the book, and changes their life, the last ten years will not have been in vain.

Alcohol will always be with us and used responsibly it is not an issue. My husband drank a bit more than most and slowly over the last eight years increased the quantities to excessive and harmful amounts. I tried every way I knew to help and support him. Doctors, counselors, hospital stays, detox units, then residential programs.

Eventually I realized he was going to drink no matter how hard I tried to "help" him. Willing and wishing he would change was useless. I could not go on living that way any longer. One day enough was enough.
When I left he had a good managerial position, nice home, family, friends and health. In two years he lost everything.

Those who live with an alcoholic partner are isolated, stressed and disheartened. The person we married is morphing into someone we don't recognize.

—

We need to know that others have trudged along the same path. Somehow there is huge relief in knowing that another person understands how we feel.

With much difficulty we need to learn to give the drinker back full responsibility for their actions and the ensuing consequences.

A few years have passed since Kevin's death.

I tried to put it all behind me, but the problems that alcohol causes are increasing. Many people can drink responsibly and it is not a problem. But for those who drink to excess and their families, it is an immense problem with no clear cut solutions.

I began to research where alcoholics could seek help if an AA/12 step program had been of no benefit for whatever reason.

That last sentence led to much more research on the subject and in turn became this, my second book. Would Kevin have approved? I will never know but if someone who is trudging along a similar path is helped, towards a healthier life I don't think he would have minded.

Education and a change in attitude is the key to the successful treatment of alcoholics. Provide these drinkers with information early. Education that they are not diseased for life and what is causing them to be like they are. They need to be empowered to turn their life around, not demoralized at every turn.

—

The goal is to interrupt the addiction cycle earlier rather than later, before chaos and destruction become the norm.

Attitudes must change. Attitudes of the general public as well as those of those treating the alcoholic. Many professionals still hold the age old view that the character of the alcoholic is flawed and they can be talked out of their dilemma. The ingrained public mindset that they are weak willed and contemptible, fuels the myths that continue to surround alcoholism. The alcoholic himself also has this ingrained belief, which over time, without education, he sees as being true. He believes he is the lowest of low, has an incurable disease that he will have forever and will never get better.

Professionals often diagnose and prescribe for the psychological symptoms of anger, anxiety, confusion, aggression, and depression, while completely ignoring the physical symptoms of alcoholism which in fact are the cause of the mental symptoms.

A change in attitude will only happen when effective treatment is seen to be working. The news of effective help will spread. By books, on the internet and by word of mouth. Families of the alcoholic will tell others how their loved one has become well.

As always the drinker must want to put effort into changing his life, but without the correct information he will stumble and fall at every hurdle.

Cherry Parker

No one sets out to be the best alcoholic they can be.

Do they think about their future in these terms: -

I will do well at school so I can get a worthwhile job.
I will buy a small house and hopefully I'll find someone to share it with. Perhaps we will have children and I will love them and provide for them.

When I am happy with what I have achieved I will increase the amounts of alcohol I consume to harmful quantities.
I will alienate my friends and family because I have become unreliable, unpredictable and unloving.

I will lose my job because my brain no longer functions normally.

I will lose my house because those who made it a home have left me and I have no work.

My health will deteriorate rapidly as I consume more and more alcohol.

Death will come too early.

No I am sure they never thought in these terms, but in a nut shell this is what can happen.

So why do some people become alcoholics and others don't?
Why do alcoholics feel compelled to drink?
Why don't they stop?
If they do stop for a while why don't they stay stopped?
Why couldn't I help my husband?
Why didn't counselors and 12 step programs help?
If he loved us why did he keep drinking?
Why did the craving for alcohol get worse over time?

Understanding why they are like they are, goes a huge way towards helping the alcoholic and the family. We who live with an alcoholic are on a roller coaster ride not of our making. We love them, we hate them, we try to help them, we don't understand what is happening and we want the good person back. Why can't he be like he used to be? Can't he see he is ruining his health? Why can't he see he is hurting us too?

This is the life I wrote about in **'Living With an Alcoholic Husband - a True Account of Living With and Without a Husband Addicted to Alcohol.**
More personal thoughts have been added here and some topics mentioned in the first book expanded on. We are somehow relieved when we understand what is happening to their brain and body. Living with them is far from easy and no alcoholic willing wants to have 'treatment.' Although if proven options are offered (one with 74% success after three years) from a sensible, logical view point it can be a good beginning.
When we have these facts we have a base from which to make honest choices. We cannot change the alcoholic ourselves, but we can offer them choices and also decide as I did whether to stay with them or leave.

For every alcoholic there is often a family standing beside them who is at a loss to know what to do. The problem has now rippled out to affect others. It has also become our problem because we care what happens to them.

We care about the physical and mental health of this person because we know who they really are when sober. We want them to return to that healthy good person we remember so we try and help them. We are looking for a golden solution to offer them as assistance.

After many years of regular drinking Kevin changed slowly before our eyes. His personality, kindness, thoughtfulness, values, high principles, the gentle person, the laughter, the hard worker, the work ethic, the hope, enjoyment and fun disappeared. It was replaced with depression, mood swings, insomnia, anger, aggression, nervousness, anxiety, fearfulness, and the inability to remember or concentrate.

The person we once knew was replaced by someone we didn't want to know. Mentally he had changed beyond recognition. Occasionally we saw little glimpses of who he used to be. But sadly these times became less and less. He became hollow and lifeless. A walking robot.

A poisonous substance in a physical body makes a physical change.

The thoughts here are all mine having lived through the problem. Use only what helps you. Every life is different and no-one's experiences will be exactly the same as mine. I left my husband twice before I said enough is enough and changed my life. He was still my best friend when he was sober, but I could not live with him. Knowing you are not alone and isolated does not fix the problem, but we are all somehow relieved to know that others are in our boat.

In this second book I have included some thoughts not mentioned before. Things I had said and other things I wish I could have said. Also included are my thoughts on the big question of treatment. I knew nothing of alternative treatment while Kevin was alive.

I am very aware that the drinker must want to change their habits and that no-one else can do that for him. They must want to do this entirely for themselves. Not because any one else wants them to. *We* know they are harming themselves, we know they can be great people when they are sober. But until they want to change for themselves alone and not because we want them to, no good will come of it.

When this time comes, options must be presented that details how others have become well and stayed that way and do not go through life struggling through each day.

The Family is involved by Default

Nothing about alcoholism is quick.

You don't wake up one morning and suddenly see an alcoholic in the room. Often I am asked when I realized my husband was an alcoholic. As if I should have been able to stab the calendar and say at 3pm on that particular day. The answer is - I don't know. Where does it begin? Like any addiction it creeps very slowly and stealthily.

In trying to maintain a normal life and helping them get back to the person they were, we the partners, are unknowingly bought in to play a large part in the drama.

The families are unwittingly involved by default. By simply being there and caring, they suffer equally as much as the addict. Statistics show that for every individual with an addiction at least ten others are directly and negatively affected.

So it stands to reason that the outcome of any treatment whether it has a positive or negative result for the individual, also impacts immensely on the family. A positive outcome helps the individual to lead a healthy sober life which in turn improves all aspects of family life.

If treatment is ineffectual the negative ripples affect the entire structure of the family. Unfortunately over time and continued drinking everything starts to unravel. Health, trust, love, respect, happiness, bank accounts and hope.

The most well-known traditional method of trying to get alcoholics back on the right path is Alcoholics Anonymous. It is recommended to the drinker by friends, doctors, hospitals and the courts. I have nothing against the fellowship of AA and it is wonderful for the individual to have found their way to a healthier, sober life through a 12 step program.

Many people have been helped in this way. However there is a poor success rate and many people have not been helped. Not everyone can relate to the teachings of a 12 step program that shames and blames while looking to a higher power for answers.

My concern is for those who are not helped by traditional methods.

What happens to them?

Where do they go now?

What happens to their families who are at a complete loss as to know what to do?

These people must be given more options for help and healing. We cannot throw the alcoholic – and the family –

on the scrap heap because they did not fit one treatment model. If we fail in helping the addict we are also failing the family. There will never be only one answer when it comes to treating an addiction.

One single type of treatment method will never be right for every single alcoholic.

One size will never fit all.

We Are All Individuals

The alcoholically dependent person has found their way to addiction slowly, by different roads and for different reasons. Over many years their actions, their history, their thoughts and choices have begun to cause imbalances in their brain and body and increasingly their life has become a mess. They have become reliant on alcohol to feel what they consider to be normal.

We each are individually who we are. A complex structure of past events, good and bad. We are shaped, by our upbringing, our choices, our fears, our dreams, physically, psychologically, environmentally, and demographically. There will never be another us.

No matter how well we think we know someone, we never really know them. We can't get into their minds, think their thoughts, prioritize their values or choose which path they follow. It is difficult enough at times to direct our own lives. So it must be that although we desperately want these drinkers to see that they are heading in a harmful direction, we cannot force them to change. We cannot make another adult do something they do not want to do. We can only offer options, choices and assistance. And there must be options to offer.

Only when they are ready to make a change themselves, will any progress be made. They may never see things the way we see them. That is just how it is. We who live with them have to accept this.

The family is often slow in realizing that no one can change the alcoholic until they themselves are ready to take full responsibility for their actions.

Sadly it takes us ages to comprehend this. We have dedicated a large chunk of our own lives trying our utmost to help this person change back into who we know they can be. Often the only solution is to change ourselves. This is not easy but in doing so the power that the addict has over the family and the control they need to hold their world together, will shift. This will be the beginning of massive change in one direction or the other.

The alcoholic's life is all about control. Control so that he can continue to live an addictive life. Unknowingly we become caught in this web because we make excuses for them. Clean up after them, drive them about, make sure they are clothed and fed, top up the bank account and we lie to ourselves.

We lie to ourselves about how bad their drinking is. We blame ourselves as if somehow we have not done enough for them and we let them run rough shod over us. We let them belittle us and put us down. We become worn down by this life. We accept it as normal. How sad we have become. We tell ourselves it is our fault. We have not done enough to help them. But it is not our fault. We must look at our problem from a different angle.

My Personal Experience

I can only write from my own personal experience. How I observed my husband who could never get his head around a 12 step program or understand the concept of a higher power. I saw him become deflated and depressed as time went on.

He used to be a lovable, kind, honest, reliable man. He was not flawed, damaged or uniquely singled out to be physiologically flawed.

All I know is that the alcohol that he continued to drink in harmful quantities eventually changed his brain. He slowly changed in front of our eyes into a completely different person. His logical thought processes disappeared.

We who live with an alcoholic partner, watch as they go to a detox centre, rehab or hospital, go to AA, drink again and then repeat the process over and over again. We do not know what to do. We watch the situation escalate. It never gets better. It only gets worse. We are dragged into it all only because we want to help.

Tunnel Vision

We befriended these people, lived with them or married them long before alcohol became so important to them. We know and love the person they were, not the person they have become, so it is only natural that we try to get that good person back. Whatever our 'normal' was has gone and we want it to return.

Life with an alcoholic seems to come with a compulsory set of blinkers. We get tunnel vision that focuses on every problem created by the drinker. Wrongly we think that if we can fix all the problems and try to keep some semblance of normality, the problem will go away.

This unfortunately is the beginning of a very long bumpy ride. This is the life I wrote about. How after many years I came to see that to get my life back I had to be the one to change.

All the while the alcoholic doesn't want our help because they see no reason to change a life they are happy with. They feel on top of what they see as a mundane world when they drink and so far alcohol is causing them no harm. The poisons they are systematically pushing into their bodies have not yet got them into any serious trouble so they see no reason to stop. They think they are invincible and have complete control of their lives. Why stop what you enjoy doing? Problem? What problem? The alcoholic sees the family as having the problem, not themselves.

Ever so slowly when the increasing amounts of alcohol change the mind and the personality, we are confronted with a new depressed version of the original person.
One who is constantly stressed, tense, on edge, never relaxed, and always surrounded by noise. They become removed from our world, annoyed, angry and frustrated. They don't want our help now either and begin to blame everybody and his brother for their problem.
It takes a long time, after much questioning, distrust, fear, disbelief, torment, anguish and heartache before we come to the conclusion that through no fault of our own we have a big problem on our hands.

Suddenly My Problem Too

This stressful situation is playing out in my own personal life – Now – this moment. It is happening to me. Not a friend, not the family next door, not the family on the TV, or along the street. It is happening to me right here in my home. It is happening to me as I sit here in my chair. How did it get this bad? Who is this person who I used to know so well?
Where has he gone?
He is standing there but it is not him.
Will he ever come back?
Will I ever get my life back to how it was?
Where will it all end?

As time goes by we not only get worn down by the problem that we have to live with every day, but we get sick and tired of it. Unknowingly we are shouldering someone else's problem while they carry on obliviously creating havoc.

Alcoholics are wonderful lovable people.
Without the alcohol.
But with the alcohol, we the partners have to deal with all sorts of rubbish. The constant lies, the broken promises, the "I'll never do it again" for the umpteenth time. The windscreen wiper effect of their moods. One minute alright, the next minute mouthy and sarcastic. The split personality of the addict is very difficult to live with. Your waking hours are spent on a knife edge trying to judge their moods.
It is an impossible task.

Their depression, self-loathing, anger, remorse, guilt, unhappiness, resentment and constant mood changes should not be ours to cope with. It all becomes too encompassing. It takes over your life. There seems to be no room for anything else.

Yes we get truly sick and tired of it. We wish we could just have some peace and quiet. The only time this happens is when they are in a hospital. What a relief that is. For a short period of time we know what a normal life can be like. Unfortunately it only lasts for a short while and we are back on the roller coaster.

But we also get angry.

When they are asking for forgiveness yet again. Asking us to believe them just one more time. Yes this time they really, really mean it. How is it going to be any different from every other time?

We get angry. We have not done anything to make them the way they are.

We can be angry if we want.

In the inevitable arguments that occurred, I said many things that were a complete waste of my breath. He never remembered what I said the next day. How I wished I could have taped these episodes to play back to him. He thought I had a vivid imagination.

Over several years some of the following I said – some I never said just wished I had.

Writing it down puts the dilemma into some perspective rather than useless words uttered to a drunken husband.

From Where I Sit

It is not all about you. We have been together a long time – for three decades. You have a nice family, a good job – why are you trying to throw it all away?

Sometimes you embarrass me. This was never how you used to be. You should not expect me to do all the day to day things while you sit there drinking yourself into oblivion. Only deigning to re-enter the world when you run out of money or when you want something. Creating misery and fear and not attempting to realize the hurt that you are causing your family.

When anything interrupts your mindset which is only focused on alcohol, you are resentful. You now live your life with alcohol as your only focus. How soon can you get to the alcohol after you finish work each night? Or counting down the hours until the weekend when you can drink uninterrupted.

You seem to fear losing control of the insulated world you have created. Can't you see that world is slowly killing you?

Retreating into your bubble and refusing to talk about why you are acting in such a sullen, uncommunicative way is not helping anyone. The only thing it is achieving is to keep us all on this merry-go-round of your making. We are going nowhere. Living this way makes me feel as though I am going mad.

Trying to talk sense to you or to ask you to see reason is impossible. When you are sober you shut down. If for a few minutes you become angry enough to be animated you rant and rave telling me I am imagining the problems and enhancing your drunken actions to make you sound worse than you are.

You are always telling me you are not hurting me. Physically no – but emotionally you are. I have tried to talk to you after you have seen counselors, but the answer you give is always the same. You say it is your problem to sort out and yours alone. You are wrong. It has become the family's problem by default. What has to happen to make you see sense?

You live in a world that is removed from everyone else. You are shutting us all out. In the past things were better, or in the future they will be better. There is no "now."

In your world "now" doesn't exist because you are always trying to maneuver the future so that it can be controlled by your odd reasoning.

To lie to your family, to look us in the face and to blatantly lie to us is demeaning. We are not dumb. You are fooling nobody with these lies. To think we don't know you have been drinking is ludicrous. You will not look us in the face. You reek of alcohol and your eyes do not focus on us. When you eventually try to look at me you focus somewhere about six inches away from my face. It takes some seconds for your brain to realize my eyes are actually above my chin.

How are you benefiting from how you are living your life now? Just going from drink to drink making sure a supply is always there. That is not a life. We are never happy anymore. We have forgotten what happiness is. Communication has gone because it needs two people.

I can't sleep properly as each night you seem to drink more. What will you do? Will you fall? When I am woken up with a loud crash what will I find? This is no way to live.

If you stay out with friends coming home whenever you like, sometimes the next day, it is apparently alright. Anything goes for you now and we are meant to ignore this. You have very different standards of behavior now. I worry that you have been in an accident or injured. Somehow you always get home and wonder why I am concerned. You think you are bullet-proof.

One day you will not be able to avoid the bullet.

You expect peace and quiet while you sleep during the day. Pity about the fact that I was awake all night thinking every car that went along the road might be you. Then once again I hear the empty apologies. The need to be forgiven as if this makes it all right and gives you a clean slate to do it all again.

You beg for forgiveness. This makes me squirm. Why put yourself in this position in the first place? It is not my place to forgive. It is your place not to do the thing you want forgiveness for. This has happened many times before. You wonder why I am hurt, baffled and distant. What do you expect? I am not proud of you when you behave like this. I don't like the way you are wandering down your own path with no regard for how you are affecting the family.

You say you are doing nothing to hurt me and I don't know when I am well off. I don't feel well off putting up with this drunken behavior. You might feel better drinking more and more but you are turning into someone we don't know. Alcohol is dissolving your values and principles. You try to manipulate me into thinking your behavior is normal. You alone are creating this mess. One day you will come out of your capsule and no-one will be there. Those who loved you will just not be able to do it anymore.

They will have had enough.

You will end up alone and lonely. Not unloved because your family will always love you, because they remember who you used to be. You are not that person anymore.

'I've learned that people will forget what you said, people will forget what you did, but people will never forget how they made you feel' – Maya Angelou

The Pretext of Normality

The façade the alcoholic needs to maintain is more difficult to keep in place as time goes by. To produce the desired effect the quantities of alcohol must be increased. All their energy is directed in keeping up a pretext of normality. Their health and memory start to suffer which only increases their fear.

The reality of throwing off this cloak of addiction and standing alone without the protection of the alcohol fills the addict with terror.
And so they retreat into what they know and once again find solace at the bottom of the bottle. Why can't they take a pill, chant abracadabra six times and their problems will evaporate? Where is the doctor with the cure?
These people are experts at avoiding situations where they have to confront personal facts. It is not in their nature and is completely foreign to them. The very nature of addiction means looking to outside influences to make things better. Using outside influences to make the problems that are inside them, better. They don't want to know that *they* might have to do something to fix their problem.
They know their life is a mess. They just want someone else to come along with the solution. Blaming everyone and everything will not make the mess go away. They alone are the only ones who can fix it. There is no point in saying they are going to get sober for any reason other than they really want their life back for themselves.
Not for the family, the wife, the partner, but for themselves alone. This will never be achieved if they think that life without alcohol will be a continual uphill struggle. Just battling through every day. If they are not going to feel any better sober - why bother?

The Great 'Why'

For us who live with these drinkers we cannot fathom why they are doing it. The fact that they don't seem to know either is baffling. Utterly baffling.

During the years of living with Kevin's drinking and since his death I have thought a lot about the WHY?
My only conclusion is that initially they must feel better in themselves with alcohol than without it.
It is as simple as that.
I am talking about a time before alcohol was doing any harm. Some use alcohol just because it makes them feel better. Better at everything. They like how they feel with alcohol instead of without it. They feel 'normal' when they drink. Others use it to cope. To cope with everyday life. They depend on an addictive substance to cope. They feel better in themselves so are able to cope. Alcohol covers sadness, despair, undetected illness and pain. It eases stress, obliterates memories, enables them sleep at night and gets them through the next day. They have got used to drinking for whatever reason in order to get to the end of the day. This has become their life.
It is why and what they are trying to cope with that is the problem.
But the alcohol works!

For a while.
Though eventually it will slowly attack them and have the completely opposite effect. The alcohol will also damage nearly all the organs in the body but mostly the brain.

Before that happens it is very easy to see why they do it and why they continue to do it. They see alcohol as the answer to feeling better in themselves. They are sure that they can do many things *better* with alcohol. Write the university papers. Stand up and deliver the speech. Visit the dying relative in hospital. Paint the house. Enjoy the party more as a there are a lot of people there they don't know. Anything to them is made better with alcohol. Never do they think or does anyone else tell them that there may be a physical reason behind the need to drink.

Why are they always nervous and tense?
Why are they depressed?
Why do they lack energy and are always tired?
Why are they always rushing around unable to relax?
Why are they moody, bad tempered, and always grumpy?
Why do they have trouble going to sleep and staying asleep?

If this is the case the answers need to be found as to why they are constantly tense, can't sleep, are depressed or whatever it is that is not right. Why do they feel not sick, but constantly below par? Has anyone ever tried to find out? Perhaps the drinker thinks that is just how they are. This harks back to my concept of individual treatment. Every one of us is different, presenting with different problems. The base line health must be examined first. And corrected. Why do they feel constantly below par?

An Unhealthy Brain

Heavy drinkers are notorious for only eating occasionally. They often have a cup of coffee and a cigarette for breakfast, don't bother about lunch, and fit dinner in between drinks. And lots more coffee. Eventually, a long way down the track, consuming food literally eats into drinking time too much and food becomes unimportant.

Many substitute alcohol for food so very little goodness enters the body.

Over time the alcoholic slowly and methodically poisons his body as well as his brain.

In very simple terms how we act, how we think, how we move, how we live, is because of billions of electric signals (neurotransmitters) going back and forth between our brain cells. These electric signals need specific chemicals to work properly and are made in the brain from amino acids that our bodies obtain each day from the protein in our food. The cells need these amino acids to function properly. Alcohol destroys these amino acids and changes the cell structure. Even a lay person can see that the lack of, or destruction of, these amino acids causes the brain to perform badly.

For the brain to be chemically balanced these neurotransmitters must be in good working order. When the brain is *chemically unbalanced* deficiencies occur and present as sleeplessness, depression, anxiety, lifelessness, brain fog and moodiness.

The main cause of neurotransmitter deficiencies are stress and poor diet. Something the alcoholic knows all about. As stress escalates the brain cannot function at the level required because of the continual reduction in amino acids.

Deficiencies can present as altered behavior and physical cravings. Extremely low levels of some neurotransmitters can cause violent behavior. Examples of some of these important neurotransmitters are endorphins (mood enhancing) dopamine (pleasure, appetite and being mentally clear) GABA (anti-stress, anti-anxiety and serotonin (promoting sleep).

This a very short example, but it can be seen how the damage is done and that repair is available. (See the book list for individual health plans and products – particularly 'Seven Weeks to Sobriety – the proven program to fight alcoholism through nutrition' by Joan Mathews-Larson, Ph.D.).

Recently the brains of alcoholically dependent people have been able to be examined by MRI scans rather than waiting for an autopsy to be completed after a painful death. These scans show that with constant drinking the brain actually shrinks.
It is not difficult to see how this person we know so well is changing into someone else. A decade ago I was not far wrong when I thought my husband needed a brain transplant to help him. With judgment and reasoning being affected the alcoholic's brain finds it hard to reason logically. The brain is literally changing. We now are looking at an unhealthy brain.

Long term it is not only the brain that is affected. The pancreas and liver struggle to cope with keeping the body in balance. The liver takes one hour to process a standard drink. A standard drink is one glass of beer, a small glass of wine or a standard serve of spirits each containing 10 mg of alcohol. The alcoholic does not drink in these delicate quantities. He often thinks in bottles rather than glasses.

Multiply this behavior over several years and we see a body and brain that have been robbed of the essential nutrients needed for physical and mental health. The stomach and oesophagus become inflamed and eventually irreversible nerve damage is seen in the hands and feet. Normal feeling is lost and replaced with constant tingly hot pain.

The muscles in the body waste away causing standing and walking to become difficult. In time the brain negates any form of pleasure and the alcoholic becomes morose and hollow. Of course this is some way down the track but it is not something to aspire to. In banking terms the body is hugely overdrawn.

Merely not drinking won't do it. If the unhealthy cells are not given nutrition and are kept malnourished, the cravings, the depression and anxiety will still be there. Not helped by the extra cigarettes, the added sweets, an overload of sugar as well as over the counter drugs to remove indigestion, migraine headaches, constant exhaustion and a general feeling of complete 'unwellness'.

To come out of the negative 'red' above average quantities of every vitamin, mineral and amino acids are needed to repair the damage.

Dr Joan Mathews-Larson's son committed suicide after trying several traditional treatment approaches for his alcoholism. She then began an intensive search for answers. Discovering it was necessary to make biochemical repairs to the body, she set about detailing her findings in the book "Seven Weeks to Sobriety". It is a must read book for anyone living with alcoholism or dealing in its treatment.

She then set up the Health Recovery Centre in 1981 and has pioneered the most successful and scientific approach available today. It has a 74% abstinence as well as freedom from cravings and unstable moods 3 years after treatment. The struggle to stay sober is removed.

The quote below is taken from "Seven Weeks to Sobriety"

"For the parents, husbands, wives and friends of an alcoholic, there is some comfort in knowing that the personality changes they have observed are a result of alterations in normal brain chemistry caused by heavy drinking. It is no more logical to blame the alcoholic for altered behavior than to demand accountability from someone with Alzheimer's disease. They don't choose to behave as they do. They are ill, victims of chemical changes they can't control.

My search for an explanation for my son's suicide finally ended when I came to understand how alcohol had affected his brain, altered his personality, and turned him into a suicidally depressed young man.

But this understanding gave rise to more questions. What could be done to prevent similar tragedies? Is there no way to undo the damage alcohol causes?

As I pondered these questions I began to wonder about the value of the conventional approach to the treatment of alcoholism. For all the spiritual resources provided by AA and the psychological insights available in counseling and group therapy, no attempts were being made to undo the damaging effects of alcohol on the delicate chemical balance that keeps the brain and central nervous system functioning normally. Why weren't we trying to fix what alcohol had broken?

The alcoholic's unstable behavior is a consequence, not a cause of alcoholism and that the personality changes stem from the physical damage done by this disease."

The reduction of these chemicals greatly affects brain activity, impacting on memory and rational thinking. Short gaps in memory are the initial symptoms and with repeated use, large blocks of memory are lost. Prolonged heavy use also causes insomnia, anxiety, impaired judgment, poor concentration, sudden mood swings, aggression, anger and depression.

What Alcohol Depletes

Alcohol interferes with many nutrients needed to keep the body functioning. These nutrients must to be absorbed from the food we consume daily.

Earl Mindell, a world renowned nutritionist states that: - *"Alcoholism is the chief cause of vitamin deficiency among civilized people with ample food supplies."* Malnutrition is caused when the empty alcohol kilojoules replace a good varied diet.

Here are just a few examples so that you can see how the alcohol consumed is negating health.

Vitamin B1 (Thiamine) converts the carbohydrates in food to energy. It helps maintain healthy nerves and may minimize the tingling and numbness in the hands and feet which is common in alcoholics due to nerve damage. It helps with digestion and keeps the nervous system and heart functioning normally. Can help with depression and anxiety attacks.

Vitamin B2 (Niacin) is necessary for a healthy nervous system and brain functions. Deficiencies cause anxiety, nervousness, fatigue and depression.

Vitamin B5 (Pantothenic Acid) is vital for the correct functioning of the adrenal glands. It is also necessary for the conversion of fat and sugar to energy. It helps to maintain a healthy nervous system. Signs of deficiency are stress and depression.

Vitamin B6. Deficiencies of this vitamin can interrupt the work of the neurotransmitters.

Vitamin B12 helps maintain a healthy nervous system. Concentration, memory and balance are improved. Deficiencies can lead to neurological disorders and depression.

Vitamin C is used up rapidly in times of stress, of which the alcoholic is under a great deal of the time. This vitamin is needed for healing and assisting the immune system.

Calcium. A lack of calcium impacts on the nervous system, causing anxiety, insomnia and irregular heartbeats. Adding Vitamin C relives tension, irritability and promotes relaxation.

Magnesium is essential for the absorption of calcium and Vitamin C. Muscles and nerves twitch and do not function smoothly when a lack of magnesium is present. Headaches occur as well as tense muscles in the torso and legs. Magnesium is known as the anti-stress mineral.

Potassium works with sodium to regulate heart beat and balance the body's hydration. Nerve and muscle function do not work well when the ratio is unbalanced. Stress in every form depletes potassium.

Zinc is present in every cell of the body and is responsible for cell growth and maintenance. It also regulates the body's acid-alkaline balance and is an important nutrient in all reproductive organs.

Inositol produces a calming effect through the body and helps maintain liver health.

Folic Acid makes blood cells, heals wounds and builds muscle. It also produces key chemicals for the brain and nervous system.

This extremely brief overview of vitamins and minerals, not to mention Vitamin A, Vitamin E, Choline, amino acids, essential fatty acids or the minerals chromium, copper, iodine, iron, manganese, selenium and others, shows what the body needs daily to maintain health. It is not difficult to see how heavy drinkers are depleting their bodies daily.

Initially a good individual nutritional plan is a must, as vitamins and minerals need to be taken in certain proportions to each other. It is useless to throw a few capsules of vitamin B1 down your throat, not feel any better and complain that yet another thing hasn't worked.

Look for good nutritional supplements from a reputable source. Not one that contains more fillers than vitamins. The old saying 'you get what you pay for' is true.

These supplements must not replace food. They need to compliment it. Although initially larger quantities will need to be taken to bring the body back into a healthy balanced state. To remain in this healthy state abstinence from alcohol and a continued repair plan may need to continue for a long time. It depends what quality of life you are seeking.

Many alcoholics consume enormous amounts of strong coffee during a day. Coffee adds to the depletion of vitamin B and ensures headaches and jumpiness. Add sugar to the equation in the form of soft drinks, sweets, chocolates and biscuits and the body has to deal with an overload of sugar.

Depression is common and symptoms are varied. They include waking up after only a few hours' sleep and being unable to get back to sleep again. Being unable to concentrate on a book or the plot of a television program. Loss of appetite and withdrawing from society as well as lack of happiness and no motivation are also symptoms.

Understanding Sugar

The amount of sugar consumed by heavy drinkers is surprising. One example can be measured by the number of drinks consumed each day that include a sweet carbonated mixer. If coke, raspberry pop or lemon fizz are added to four drinks a day this puts 36 teaspoons of sugar into the body. 252 teaspoons over one week and just a little over 1000 teaspoons a month. A whopping 48kg or 105lb of sugar per year. All from 4 drinks a day with a mixer. It's quite a lot of sugar that the body is trying to deal with.

85% - 95% of alcoholics are hypoglycemic and don't know it. Hypoglycemia is when the glucose/blood sugar (same thing) in the blood is too low.

Drinking alcohol raises the blood sugar level. The pancreas begins to put insulin into the blood to lower the blood sugar level. In people who are not hypoglycemic this would balance the levels. Unfortunately for those who are hypoglycemic the pancreas goes into overdrive making the levels too low. Symptoms such as shakiness, weakness, nervousness, a light headed feeling, irritation, difficulty in concentrating and heart palpitations are just some of the feelings.

The liver and adrenal glands now come into play, trying to raise the blood sugar levels. More unpleasant feelings occur such as sweating, chronic anxiety and gasping for air. When all this panic and stress begins, the alcoholic drinks to alleviate all the horrible symptoms. Alcohol is seen as the answer as it does the trick for a short time but the cycle repeats and repeats.

In fact the answer lies in treating the hypoglycemia and addressing the consumption of what is causing it to happen.

With each repetition the liver, the pancreas and adrenal glands become increasingly stressed causing the person to be exhausted and constantly feeling in the need of a 'pick me up.' Alcohol being the depressant that it is and not the 'pick me up' as is often thought, puts the drinker in a no win mess.

Abstaining from alcohol will still leave the liver, adrenals, pancreas and other organs stressed and weakened – and the cravings for the alcohol and sugar will still be there.

J Mathew-Larson's book explains this common problem very clearly giving instructions for repair. When an alcoholic stops drinking and the above symptoms occur it has been labeled 'dry drunk syndrome.' It seems very strange these symptoms are identical to hypoglycemia. We can now see how large a part sugar plays in the alcoholic's health or rather lack of it.

An Automatic Response

Drinking has become an automatic response to *any* stress. Before any thought can be given to a solution the arm is already extending towards alcohol. These habits and automatic responses need to be recognized and addressed.

New tools need to be put in place to deal with inevitable stress. New skills and nutrition must be taught and practiced. These plans must to be tailored to the individual as each comes with their own unique set of problems.

When physical reconstruction and repair are maintained then any psychological issues can be addressed from a far healthier platform. The brain and body can begin to recover.

Peace of Mind

We cannot give away peace of mind. We cannot buy peace of mind. The doctor can't write a prescription for it and the more we look outside ourselves for it, the more it becomes unattainable.

People dependent on alcohol are always looking for the quick answer. Cut the babble and waffle just get to the bottom line. The quick solution. They don't want the personal upheaval that is needed for change to happen nor do they want to take the time.
For each of us to obtain peace of mind for ourselves we must ask ourselves some hard questions and also answer them truthfully. These questions are detailed in my first book so will not be repeated here.

My husband often said all that he wanted was peace in his mind. I could not give that to him. Nor could the doctor, no one could. But he could never see that to truthfully confront the things that were wrong in his life could mean a beginning towards a personal truth and an inner peace.
This is not wimpy, mushy or something men don't do, it is just plain honesty. People will be only too happy to help you if you are looking to improve.

However, alcoholics are always trying to fool themselves and so they think, other people. Little do they realize that they are very transparent.

Peace of mind will never be achieved unless the things that are causing the distress are confronted. Whether it is physical or mental. This goes for the alcoholic and those living with them. No problem is ever solved by ignoring it.

Inner Turmoil

There comes a time when they really do want to stop drinking. But they want someone else to tell them how to do it – and quickly. Or they feel the need to tough the problem out themselves.

After time it seems as though there are two people fighting in their head. One knowing they are getting nowhere and could with some effort on their part get out of this quagmire. The other voice is yelling that it is just too hard.

If they have another drink these two noisy opposing viewpoints will fade away. But only for a while. Then they will sober up and bang – the voices are still there. Yelling about the same old problems but louder this time as another drinking episode has been added to the mix. Worrying about what they did this time and can't remember.

All this inner turmoil takes some time to build. None of it happens overnight. That is why addiction or dependency is so slow and insidious.

We, who live with them, can now see the addiction escalating as the alcoholic desperately seeks to cover up this inner turmoil. As the quantities of alcohol increase so do the lies, the arguments, the lack of respect and the fear the drinker now feels.

It is Just How I Am

An alcoholic hell bent on staying on his soggy path is not too keen on any truth. It is shied away from at any cost. They see everyone else as having an easier life and they alone have been singled out to carry a heavier burden.

The fact that other males on my husband's family were also heavy drinkers is the first excuse.
We have yet to find a specific alcoholic gene, just as we don't have an honesty gene or a murderous gene.
Yes they may have a tendency towards alcohol as others have a tendency to breast cancer or asthma or heart disease. If you had a mother or an aunt who had had breast cancer wouldn't you seek out any new medical therapeutic advice to help you be as good as you could be with the knowledge of today?
You can't undo a tendency but you can learn how to manage your own health in the best way possible. Perhaps they have inherited the same brain chemicals as the parent. Could a nutritional imbalance have been inherited? If the parent was deficient in some brain chemical perhaps they are too.
Scotland has become the first place in Europe to prescribe a new drug, nalmefene, which reduces cravings for alcohol by reducing the release of dopamine in the brain, lessening the reward sensation associated with the drink. Trials of the drug have shown men who normally drank eight units of alcohol a day and women who drank six units of alcohol a day drank half as much over a six month period after taking the drug.

It must also be remembered that it is not only those born with certain biochemical vulnerabilities that become alcoholics. A biochemical change can also develop later in life from continued drinking whether the parent is an alcoholic or not.

Seemingly knowledgeable people will nod their heads wisely when they hear that any relative of an alcoholic has also had a drinking problem. As if they have written them off already as being incurable and always branded an alcoholic. With this reaction the negative thinking of the drinker is reinforced and his beliefs confirmed.

Our genes are not a blueprint for our lives that we have to follow to the letter. No doubt if any of us went back among the branches of our family trees we would find a heavy drinker. Often well hidden by the family under the disguise of an illness. Individual environment, choices, ill health, reaction to stress and a positive or negative outlook on life all come into play. A personal decision to work through problems rationally and logically, or rush to self-medicate immediately in order to cope? We are all different.

They tell themselves that this is just how they are and they will never be any different. I was born this way. Why did it have to happen to me? They continue to judge themselves with every drinking episode. Seeing themselves as having failed again and again and judging themselves accordingly. Shame and disappointment are added to the mix.

They choose to decide this is how they will always be and take on a victim mentality. They become happy to wallow in what they see as an unfair birthright. It is the best excuse to stay stuck in their problem and not look for another way out. Any failed treatment in the future will reinforce this viewpoint.

An incorrect personal belief is becoming engrained and confirmed repeatedly. Each drinking episode confirms it. They never question the fact that their own beliefs may be totally incorrect. As time goes by they meet other people in rehab centers and at group meetings who also hold this belief. So it must be true. Others think the same as they do. We are now at the point when they say "You don't know what it's like. You don't understand me."

Not Happy People

These heavy drinkers are generally not happy people. In a crowd they give the appearance of being happy souls but alcoholism is all about appearances.

Probably not a good metaphor to use, but some of us see life as the glass being half full and others are convinced it is always half empty. If we see the world as sad, unhealthy, difficult, incomprehensible, unfathomable place, with constant uphill struggles that is how we will venture into it.

Some find it very difficult to see another picture. They are surprised when something good happens to them. For some reason the belief is held that it is not deserved.

Belief here is the word that keeps cropping up. It must be remembered that not all our beliefs are correct. Just because they are yours or your families they may not be correct. These beliefs are the opinions you hold. Sometimes passed down from generation to generation. That is how it always has been. Never questioned. Other beliefs may not be wrong they may merely be different.

Many people have set beliefs and never challenge them. They are not open to discussion. They believe whatever, because that is how they have always thought and nothing is going to change it. No, you don't have to change what you believe, but you can be open to other opinions that may be helpful to you.

41

There was no way my husband would have stopped and listened to the above when he was drinking. Vitamins and minerals in an individual health plan to help with alcoholism? He would have been extremely skeptical. Perhaps he wouldn't have been so skeptical with a 74% success rate. Maybe in sober times he would have taken notice, but his body and brain had become too sick and hope had disappeared.

When you have lost hope you have lost everything.

When Kevin was alive I did not know of the options I have outlined here. Whether it would have been of benefit we will never know. But it would have provided options. Choices to be pondered.

Alcoholics have tunnel vision. They see nothing but the drink at the end of the tunnel. And are hell bent on getting there no matter what. They don't see that the family is suffering. We become blurred side issues. They become enclosed in their own impenetrable bubble. With an eye firmly focused on some euphoric, unreachable, invisible future they drink steadily not caring about anything. Alcohol in time becomes more important than life.

It Is Easy To Understand

It is very easy to understand how the body and brain have been changed. We also may realize that if they do become sober for some time why they drink again, as the reason, the main cause has not been addressed. Maybe they *are* depressed, out of balance and unwell. But reading and knowing what is happening to them does not make it any easier to live with. Would he put up with it if it was me doing

the drinking? In a sober time I put this question to him. The answer – "No I wouldn't have stayed. I would have been long gone."
Mmmmmmm.

We are told they can't help themselves and the illness is to be separated from the person. I find this impossible to do. Yes they have made themselves ill from drinking more and more and more. We see them ruining their health every day. The problem escalates with every empty glass. They themselves will even say it is doing them harm. They realize after some years that their brain is not as sharp and their life is heading down a slope. But they continue to drink.

It is a problem that really messes with your head and it is exceedingly difficult to keep living on the roller coaster of emotions day after day, year after year. You really do feel like a hamster on a wheel, getting off occasionally to bang your head against a brick wall.

The once cheerful, rational, endearing person we used to know, morphs into someone who is bad tempered and constantly critical. Someone who torments, plays drunken mind games and makes you feel as though you are somehow to blame for their predicament. We hear the argument again and again, that it is not their doing. The fault always lies with someone else or it is just how they are. They will tell us that 'you don't know when you are well off' and 'what are you complaining about – I'm not doing you any harm.' Not yet they're not, but you never know.

It goes on and on. Doubt creeps into your mind. Perhaps it is not as bad as you think. (Oh yes it is!)

Being surrounded by constant negativity can wear anybody down. We become sapped of energy and deflated in spirit. Wrongly believing it *is* somehow our doing. We keep on hoping that the next doctor or counselor or hospital will make him see sense. The truth is that the only time you feel as if you have any energy to call on is when they have sobered up and are promising never to do it again.

In their now pitiful state our energy slowly returns in the hope that maybe this time they really will stay sober – at least for a while. How sad is that?

They are promising to be nice, asking for forgiveness again and saying they can't manage without us. Living with an alcoholic year after year, we slowly unknowingly absorb their negativity. We lose the energy and inspiration to try new things and think new thoughts, because keeping up a semblance of normality uses all the energy we possess. We wake up tired because sound sleep is impossible. Always on the alert, ready for the next catastrophe. Half the time waking up in fear.

Fear because they haven't come home. What has happened this time? Has there been an accident? Have they been arrested? Where are they? If the truth be known having the time of their lives not giving a care in the world about you.

When you are in the whirlpool of a problem it is difficult to see how far down you are being sucked.

Happiness.......What Happiness?

We, who live with alcoholic partners, are not happy people either. We don't smile much and laugh less. We look enviously at other people who seem to be content with what they choose to do. They smile and laugh – not false smiles that stay on their teeth, but ones that reach all the way up to their eyes. Most likely they have problems too, but I don't think they dread evenings and most of all weekends.

Passing a couple in the street comfortably chuckling about a shared happy moment you are suddenly struck by the thought – 'When did we last laugh like that?'

Give that question some real thought and it is sad to think how long ago it was. You forget what being happy was like. You forget what enjoying precious moments were like. They just don't happen.

The alcoholic has been unhappy for so long they think it is the normal way to feel. The partner has also slowly and unknowingly forgotten what happiness is.

There is no laughter anymore.

A Need to Cope

Every addiction comes from a need to cope with something. There is always a reason why they feel they need alcohol to compensate for the times they feel inadequate. To begin with the alcohol gives them the confidence they lack, makes them feel more at ease with people, numbs emotional and physical pain, adds stamina and just makes them feel better in general.

The USA Substance Abuse and Mental Health Services Administration (SAMHSA) program has recently said "There is no question that alcoholism is a disease *process*. There are some behaviors associated with getting started that tend to be voluntary in the beginning but very quickly become the disease process. We must stay focused on this disease process of alcoholism which is not unlike other diseases – diabetes for example and it needs to be treated that way."

They succeed for years, and maybe decades go by while they maintain the façade at work and at home. The picture many have of a derelict person on a park bench drinking from a bottle wrapped in a brown paper bag is not your average alcoholic.

These drinkers are intelligent everyday people often holding responsible jobs, shopping in your supermarket, sitting next to you on the bus or train, at the office, or living next door. Managers, mothers, hairdressers, doctors, postmen, engineers, butchers, bakers and policemen. Anyone you want to name.

Myths

Alcoholics have a flawed character.
Alcoholism *becomes* a brain disease. The body and brain change with the continued excessive consumption of alcohol. They are not flawed in their character or personality.

Alcoholics need to reach rock bottom before they can accept help.
This is simply not true. The earlier good help and care can begin the better.
These alcoholics can bump and stumble along the rocky bottom for years making regular appearances in hospitals, police cells and courts.

Alcoholics don't have any willpower. They can stop if they really want to.
The heavy drinking starts slowly but over time the continued use changes the way the brain functions.
The brain then begins relating messages that it needs more of that substance to operate, making them crave alcohol even more. And so making it increasingly difficult for the person to quit.

Alcoholics need to be punished.
The punishment approach is used in some residential programs. They are asked to see what they have lost and will lose by drinking. They are told their health will deteriorate. Even when told they are slowly killing themselves with every drink they don't stop. Scrubbing more pots and pans will go no way to helping them.

Words

Henry Ford did and said many clever things. Here are two of his quotes that are special.

'Whether you think you can, or you think you can't – you will be right.'

'Failure is simply an opportunity to begin again – this time more intelligently'

Words can make us think and uplift us or they can make us think and depress us.

Try these words and see how uplifted you feel: -

'This is a disease you will have for life'
'Once an alcoholic, always an alcoholic'
'You must hit rock bottom'
'You are powerless'
'Recovery is forever'
'You have made bad decisions'
'This will be the first of many residential stays'
How uplifted would you feel if a doctor or therapist said these things about whatever you had wrong with you? You would either lose all hope and visibly deflate and say –

'I knew all along no-one could help me' – or you would run out the door in search of better treatment.

If you have talked yourself into being the best failure you can be, your mind will create every opportunity to enforce that belief. On the other hand if you have decided to better yourself a positive belief will produce positive experiences. Look for alternative choices to help you in the right direction.

Co-Dependents and Enablers

More negative words. The dictionary definition of enabling is to give authority or means to make possible.
Codependency is defined as living through or entirely for, another person. Taking on the blame for their drinking, trying to fix their problems and taking care of their every need. A relationship in which a person is controlled or manipulated by another, often involving placing a lower priority on one's own needs. Caring is not enabling. Wanting to help is not enabling. Surely enabling and codependency, if they truly exist, are making an environment where the addiction can continue uninterrupted.

To label those who live with an addicted person this way is wrong. We stay and help because we care and want to see them get better. Even when our efforts seem to be in vain we are not enabling. It is not your fault or anything you did or didn't do that causes them to drink. Nothing you can do or say will stop them quickly. There is no sudden solution to an addiction of any kind.
Threats, yelling, whispering, bargaining or blackmail will not do the slightest bit of good. They will keep drinking until

they choose to do otherwise. How long this will take is anyone's guess. It may never happen.

Just as you didn't start the drinking, you alone can't end it. Often for any change to occur, you, the partner will have to be the one doing the changing.

A good exercise is to go back in your mind two, five, or even ten years. Step back and look at your life with the drinker then. What was it like? What were the dreams and aspirations?

Now look at the life you have now. What would you have thought then of the life you are leading now? What would you have truthfully thought?

The trouble is that the problems and life with an alcoholic change so slowly, so very slowly, we do not realize how bad it is actually getting.

If only we could stand back for a few days, away from the mess and look at it calmly and clearly we would be astonished. Why are we putting up with all this horror?

The main reason is when they are sober we hope, always hope, that perhaps this time they will stay that way. The intervals of seeing that good sober person keep us convinced that one day they will emerge and stay as the person we used to know.

It takes us a long, long time to realize we may have lost that person for good. We become exhausted, confused, and torn between what we know is right and what we are confronted with. How long do you have to wait for that person to return? Will they ever return? Meanwhile we are plodding along beside them trying to make them see sense. But they don't want to know.

The stress I felt is a result of my husband's actions when he drinks. There is a simple reason why I can't breathe properly, can't sleep properly, am anxious, fearful and constantly wish I was somewhere else. The stress is because of his drinking that I didn't cause. I have done everything to help him. In sober times he would agree. He even put this into a speech after a 12 week residential program.

"Over the years I was lucky enough to have a loving wife who could not do more for me. To Cherry, thanks for everything".

So enabling – no.

Something Has to Happen

Just as something caused these good people to drink in the first place and helped them to cope, often something has to happen before any thought is given to reversing it. Why would they stop if their health, finances, families, or life style has not, in their eyes be affected. Why bother to stop doing something they enjoy doing? Certainly not because someone in their family wants them to.

A wake up call can come in the form of a car accident. Hopefully not involving injury to an innocent party. Or being left alone to cope for themselves. I believe when things have become so difficult as to affect the health of others in the family the alcoholic needs to be left. Not forever but for a short time. Time to hopefully sort themselves out. They must stay alone until the family has proof that they are heading in the correct direction and not merely promising to do so. This wakeup call can sometimes be what is needed to see the true picture. Something bad normally happens if the problem goes on for too long.

'Treatment'

An introduction towards any type of 'treatment' is normally raised the first time a medical person appears on the scene. Sometimes in the form of their own doctor, but it could also be as the result of a hospital admission. Police intervention and court appearances are waiting further down the track. By the time their own doctor is consulted it is often for medical reasons caused by the excessive consumption of alcohol. Treatment is then provided for the symptoms of this excess, for example faulty digestion and gout, not the cause.

If the alcoholic is deemed to need medical detoxing over a seven day period the family see this as a solution. They think their loved one is going to get the necessary treatment and all will be well. How wrong they are. This is just the beginning. The road will only get bumpier.
After sobering up in a detox facility or hospital the person is then given back to the family, told to see their personal doctor and to attend AA meetings. The families are at a complete loss to know what to do. Is this all that is going to be done?

Often the person they get back is also dumbfounded, has lost a lot of confidence, is embarrassed, ashamed and oddly seems to have suddenly lost many coping skills.

And so they come to AA and a 12 step program, thinking that those running the sessions know best. Sure in the knowledge someone can tell them how to become sober. They know they need to stop drinking. But now they are at the stage that they don't know how.

The ordinary person in the street has no reason to know anything about treating addictions. It has not featured in our lives so we don't think about it. The engrained public view is that alcoholics are getting *treatment* by going to an AA/12 step program. This is not the case. It is a support group where other alcoholically dependent people meet and remain sober with the help and support of other members. It is not professional treatment.

We know nothing about the poor success rate of traditional treatment.

The statistics and text below are taken from the book – **AA Not the Only Way** written by Melanie Solomon. Her father was helped by AA but Melanie was unable to find the answers at AA for herself and nearly died. She became sober after a nine year battle with addiction and now devotes her life to researching recovery options.

"AA's internal results from five surveys from 1977 – 1989 yielded the following numbers.

81% of attendees are gone after 1 month – 19% remain
90% attendees are gone after 3months – 10% remain
93% attendees are gone after 6 months – 7% remain
95% are gone at the end of the year – 5% remain"
Only 5%.

They come to AA with the preconception that others also have, that this is treatment. As stated before many people have been helped by these meetings. I am concerned with those who have not.

Does everyone feel comfortable standing up in front of a group of strangers and declaring themselves to be an alcoholic? Do they feel demoralized, intimidated, scared and uncomfortable? I'm sure they do. Is this helping them?

They have also had the image in their mind of the alcoholic, as we all have, of the unkempt and disheveled tramp going through rubbish bins. Now that stigma is being put onto their shoulders. And an ingrained stigma it will become. In their by now depressed state, they begin to think they really are second rate citizens. They are ashamed and are losing self-esteem. On arriving home the family asks how they got on. Sure in the knowledge they have begun treatment.

The mindset of most is, if the drinker fails to become a sober citizen we somehow think that they are at fault. Perhaps they did not try hard enough, didn't stick it for long enough or didn't really want to stop. We never question the system. And it is forgotten about it because unless it is in our family, it is not our problem.

It is not until we are confronted with an alcoholic in our own home that we come face to face with the 'treatment' of today.

If you want to become fit you may join a gym. After a while you realize this is not for you. The members are too young, too old, the music is too loud. It just isn't you. Perhaps you are happier with another gym, a personal trainer or maybe you just want to get fit with your exercycle in the basement.

If you want to get thinner you might join a weight reduction program. In time if you find you are not comfortable you have the choice to try another company, go to see a personal nutritionist or dietician or lose weight your own way.

If you want to become sober you are directed to an AA meeting or a 12 step program. Maybe you are not suited to turning your problem over to a higher power and being told you are powerless over your choices.

Just because the methods that a 12 step program advocates don't fit with you, it doesn't mean you have **failed**. It means you are one of those who have not found your answers with this one type of assistance for alcoholics.

If you "fail" at AA more guilt and hopelessness is heaped onto the already growing pile. It is said that the individual is "not ready" to become sober. How can this be said to an already demoralized and confused person?

If one method of 'treatment' has not been successful do we throw the alcoholic, and their family who are equally affected out on the compost heap?

No we need to be able to offer choices.

Vacovsky, the Executive Director of the American Council on Alcoholism, May 12, 2005 wrote – "Many, if not most alcohol dependant individuals have lost faith in themselves, and more importantly hope for the future. It is common for such individuals to have numerous attempts at sobriety, most often using 12-step methods. They have been programmed to accept themselves as hopeless and powerless, with their chance of recovery being slim to none. It is up to the individual to determine what the most appropriate treatment is. It is up to the treatment community to provide options that set up individuals to succeed, rather than be expected to fail."

Different Types of Alcoholics

As a 12 step program will not suit all alcoholics, so one biochemical nutritional program cannot meet every need.
Both Dr Gant (former medical director of Tully Hill hospital in New York) and Joan Mathews-Larson work in the fields of treating biochemical imbalance in the brain with nutritional supplements. 'Seven Weeks to Sobriety' details the different nutrients needed for the at least four alcoholic types.

For example there is the alcoholic who feels invigorated with alcohol, can drink everyone else under the table and does not often get hangovers. Later in life his health will suffer and he won't feel better by drinking. He will feel the opposite as the alcohol is now killing him. This person's liver processes alcohol differently to other people.

Some are ill the first few times they try alcohol, but persevere to fit in with the crowd and in time become used to it. Craving escalates with age.

Nearly all Mathews-Larson's patients are hypoglycemic but are unaware that this is a large part of their problem. The difference of psychological and biochemical depression is also discussed where she describes the seven different types of depression that present at her clinic. Each type needs an individual health plan, which she lists, as well as detailing why.
You will be able to see that alcohol addiction is not only helped in many different ways but also comes from many different sources.

Time and Cost

Many may say that the cost of individualized counseling and personalizing a nutritional plan will be too great. Yes that may be so. With no guarantee at the end.

There are few guarantees in life. We do not guarantee a 100% cure for cancer, diabetes, or asthma but we do the best with what we have and what we know at the time. The cost of fuelling an addiction of any kind as it inevitably escalates, will be extremely expensive over a lifetime. As will the public cost in ambulance fees, hospital admissions, court appearances and the police presence. Not to mention the loss of trust, respect, dignity, self-worth, friendship and marriages. A myriad of things that money can't buy.

Those dependent on alcohol are by nature, people who want a quick fix to most things. They are not tolerant of waiting some time to get an answer. It has taken years to get to where they are today, so in turn it cannot be expected that health will be returned tomorrow. As they have put time and money into becoming unwell, so their time and money must be invested to reverse the process.

Effort needs to be put into recovery. Not just looking at nutrients in a bottle and hoping. Not just looking at good food while eating candy. Not consuming a large container of coffee while reading the book.

Planning to climb Everest wasn't done on a whim and a 'just let's do it' moment. Much planning and training to get fit was involved. You could not just grab a sweatshirt and begin. So effort and actually doing something must go into it. Read one of the recommended books and see how others have achieved sobriety through nutritionally healing the damaged cells. Don't knock it till you try it. 74% achieving sobriety with no cravings after three years is better than 12% helped by going to a support group and doing it one day at a time. Give it a go. It might save your life.

The brain and body need to begin to come back into balance before counseling will be of use. Do both. Make the biochemical/nutritional repairs and then add the psychological therapy. Do them both together - but do something.
When you do look for counseling, if you need it, make sure you find a good qualified therapist who is knowledgeable in current help for alcohol addiction. Shop around, there are some cowboys out there masquerading as experts.

In two different clinics I was told that I knew my husband well enough to know when he was going on a drinking binge and should be able to talk him out of it. Another suggested I water down the vodka. They had no idea.

Reading from a text book as to how to help an alcoholic is a very different thing to having lived every day with their mentality. Doctors and counselors can walk away from their offices at the end of the day leaving their patients problems in the filing cabinet. Find a counselor who really knows what they are talking about.
Good professional honest counseling is a must because the reason that they are self-medicating needs to be found. Otherwise it will be back on the rollercoaster.

The Medical Profession

Since Kevin's death I have read many books and looked for help other than a 12 step program, as there must be others who have not been helped by traditional methods.
The drinkers are often too sick in mind and body and defeated in spirit to put any energy into finding another option for help. They have thought like many in the population that a 12 step program was treatment, because everybody, medical people included have told them it is so.

With such a poor success rate why are more alternatives not being tried?
Don't expect many in the medical profession to guide you towards any type of holistic help. Natural methods of returning to health and medical minds don't mix. This is not what they have trained for. You will be laughed out of their rooms as if you had suggested a comical cure. They seldom acknowledge that another opinion as to how to heal may lie outside their medical boxes. Drug companies don't peddle vitamins and minerals that are unable to be patented.
Medicine has its place and we are grateful that it has progressed so far in many areas, but the treatment of alcoholism is not one of them.

Change

Change means giving up what we know and are comfortable with and setting forth into unknown territory. People fear change because it is generally thought that what we don't know is going to be negative. Why is that? Why won't it be better? We are comfortable with what we know and we become afraid to change.

How many people do you know who are in jobs they hate but won't look for something better? They spend all their time moaning and groaning about the pay, the annoying workmates, the inconsiderate boss. Others stay in marriages that they constantly complain about. Often putting the partner down and explaining how they would have had a better life with someone different. They are always talking behind the partner's back about leaving but never do. These moaners choose the people they complain to. People who can do nothing about their predicament.

They do not like to move out of their comfort zone and actually do something to make their life better. They would rather wallow around in their sad prisons complaining constantly but doing nothing.

Change can often mean confrontation. It is easier to do nothing. Easier to walk away and moan to someone else than confront the problem and look for a solution. Change means getting up and physically moving in the right direction.

Everyone who wants to change must want it for themselves. The alcoholic must want the freedom from addiction enough to change his life for himself alone. Not because anyone else wants him to.

I believe changes need to be made in the drinker's attitude and thoughts as well as to the places he has up until now, led his life. They cannot tread the same paths with all the same friends and habits looming at every turn. New interests must be sought. Good true friends will stay and help.

When they remove the drinking there is a lot of time to fill in. They need to realize there is a world over the rim of the glass, with many things in it to be done. What have they always wanted to do? What interests them? Their life has been lived with a drink in their hand or thinking about the next drink in their hand. There actually is a world out there. It is a very different place to their restricted prison. In other words they must begin to piece together a new life. Because an alcoholic doesn't have a life. They merely exist from one drink to the next.

You can't cross a sea by merely staring into the water – R Tagore

Don't count the days. Make the days count. – Muhammad Ali, boxer

The journey of a thousand miles must begin with a single step.
- Lao Tzu, Chinese philosopher

Choices

My first book – '**Living with an Alcoholic Husband.' A true account of living with and now living without a husband addicted to alcohol**, offered choices as to whether to stay with the alcoholic or leave. Much soul searching must happen on both sides but I believe they do need to be left for a time. Left to fend for themselves but communication still needs to be maintained - when they are sober. When things get too bad it is very difficult to comprehend the problem from within the turmoil. We all have different circumstances so we must choose what is best for us.

This second book offers choices on how to get to a healthier state and maintain it. We now have scientific proof that alcohol in time does damage and change the brain dramatically. Like many illnesses, if we catch this early enough, less damage will have been done and the sooner health can be restored.

How the alcoholic, how everybody, has chosen to react to what life has dealt them, has got them where they are today. It is now up to them to choose positively or negatively where to go from here. We all have choices to make. Ham or cheese. Blue shirt or white. Improvement or the same old stuff. If they are satisfied with how things are now they won't do anything. They will stay stuck. If stuck does it for them that is where they will stay. Stuck with a glass in their hand. All the way to the cemetery.

Change means you have to do something. You have to physically do something towards what you want.

Dependency on alcohol comes initially from masking something that is difficult to cope with. It is used as a survival tool. Then it compounds as time goes by because the alcohol itself becomes an added problem. Until this mask is removed no headway will be made.

It involves work on their part. Alcoholics want others to do the work regarding their health, for them. They often work hard in many other areas of their life, but this personal problem needs them to face the fact *they* need to work towards better health in their own brain and body. This is what they have been avoiding. The drinker must want to get well for themselves. To want the freedom and peace of mind badly enough.

Riding Uphill

We, who live with these drinkers, know that without the alcohol they are wonderful people. Sadly they do not think that of themselves. Alcoholism is indeed a huge problem and does not always have a happy ending. We can suggest the good counseling, suggest why their health is deteriorating and how they could help themselves but sometimes it does no good.

It is difficult to remember that we cannot make anyone live their life the way we want them to live it. Then it would be our life. They have their life and we can only encourage them to seek alternative treatment if one method has not been successful. Perhaps they won't see it our way. None of us likes to be told what to do. The future will unfold one way or the other. We sometimes have to face the fact that it may not be the future we saw in our mind. That's just how it is.

After reading my first book Linda wrote to me describing her life with an alcoholic partner. Her story is different to mine, just as everyone else's will be different. Her analogy of riding a bike uphill is great way of describing our lives.

With her permission: here is her story.

"When you're sitting on a rollercoaster, you hold on tight. The last thing you feel like doing is jumping off it; you think that the landing will kill you, and you might be right – then again, you could be wrong. It will hurt, but you might just survive it. That's what happened to me. I jumped because I was left with no choice. I came to realize that if I stayed on this rollercoaster that I would die, both emotionally and spiritually. So I jumped, knowing that I had a better chance of living, than if I stayed. The landing was painful, but I am recovering from the injuries I sustained, and I am able to get up and walk away from it.

—

Living with an alcoholic is bizarre and painful. It's an existence based on hope and not a lot else. I had hoped to retrieve the man I fell in love with, but he had long gone into some sort of dark pit of his own making. Not only that, he was doing his very best to drag me into it with him. Luckily there was something in me that refused to take the final leap into that dark place.

To get out of a relationship like this takes some doing. It isn't easy. In my case, I was in a very difficult situation. We were living in a house which I had bought with my own money. He never paid anything towards the cost of keeping the house – I paid the mortgage, the rates, insurance, the whole lot. He kidded himself that he was working from home as a web designer. I was the one going out to work. All he did was drink. In an email he had assured me he would be happy to sign a contract to enable me to protect my assets before I had bought the house, and foolishly I believed him. Of course, once we were in the house, he refused. He'd got what he wanted. From the time we moved into that house, he used to use his entitlement to half of it as a way to keep me quiet. He had some serious leverage. I had put a lot of money into the place when I bought it so I stood to lose many thousands of dollars. He seemed to get a lot of pleasure in the power that this gave him. The verbal abuse became more and more hurtful; the verbal abuse eventually, and inevitably, became physical. He had me over a barrel and he knew it. This was a bumpy rollercoaster ride.

He became sicker and sicker; it got to the point where he wouldn't even bother going to the toilet, he'd just throw up over the banister of the deck onto the garden, and then just carry on drinking. He kept crazy hours – it was a 24 hour cycle of drink for maybe 8 hours, pass out for 4 to 6 hours, then up again, drinking for another 8 hours or so. This meant that he was up at all hours of the night while I was trying to sleep because I had to work the next day. I tried to get his family to join with me to help him – he had 5 siblings. Addiction is entrenched in his family. G's father was an alcoholic. His younger brother died at a young age due to drink and drugs. His sister has a drink problem which has put her relationship at serious risk. His older brother tried to talk to him. Even his sister offered to stop drinking with him and attend AA. Nothing helped and they just gave up. I went to counseling and the counselor suggested that I somehow inject his cask of wine with water to dilute it.

I didn't go back to that counselor.

The end came quite suddenly. One night he just turned around to me and said "how much will you pay me to get out of your life?" I looked at him. The question had come out of nowhere and I had to make a decision. Would I do what I had done so often before and tell him that I had no intention of breaking off the relationship, that nothing had changed, that I still cared for him and wanted to be with him, just so that I would get some peace in the house and so there would be no shouting, no name calling, no danger? Or would I bite the bullet and follow my heart? I looked at him. In his face I saw the misery, the self-hatred, the sorrow. I couldn't remove any of it. There was nothing I could do for him now. I had tried and tried and it was time to look after myself. I asked him how much he was thinking of. And so I made the leap off the rollercoaster into the void. There followed 7 months of hell. Lawyers got involved because he refused to leave the house even though I had offered to help meet the costs of moving; he became so abusive that I had to eventually go to court to get a protection order and occupation order against him. It took months. Thank God we have no children. I would hate to drag children through all this, but it also meant that I was a low priority as far as the Family Court was concerned. I hung on at home. Every night was a special kind of torture, not knowing what he'd do next. The drinking made his behavior unpredictable and particularly nasty. He would taunt me with tales of what he was going to do with all the money that I'd have to give him. He'd yell at me calling me anything from a whore, a slut, a psycho, the list goes on. I had to leave the house for a month because it was too much of a nightmare living there. I was confused, desperate and helpless.

Work was a sanctuary for me. I continued to perform well there because although my colleagues didn't know the whole story, they did know enough about my situation to realize that it was unpleasant. The support I got was amazing. Most of it was subtle, wordless support. It should not surprise anyone that I work with women. I felt safe there.

My girlfriends were an unbelievable network of strength around me. G had tried his best to isolate me from them, but had never quite succeeded. I advise any woman in any kind of abusive relationship never, ever to allow their partner to alienate them from their friends. In a situation where a person is involved with an alcoholic, it's very easy to become isolated as the nature of the addiction is such that it needs an enabler, a person that unquestioningly supports the addict. Having friends outside the situation puts the addict at risk of having his or her addiction confronted and questioned, not something he or she wants.

The judge sat on the bench on June 4th, the day of the protection order hearing and said that he had never come *across anything like this before, and ordered G out of the house on June 6th. That day is etched in my mind forever. After the hearing G tried to negotiate, cajole, threaten and manipulate me into giving him "a few more days" to get out of the house but now that I had the backing of the court, I refused. It felt so good after so many years of feeling so weak. I said no to him time and time again. On June 6th, I came home from work and the house was quiet. It was peaceful. It was a Friday, so I had the weekend to wander around the house, getting to know it again after having stayed in motels. I cleaned. On Monday I had the locks changed. On Tuesday I sent all his stuff to his mother's house, where he had gone. I have not heard from him directly, although litigation is ongoing. I could still lose this house. But what I have gained is worth far more than all the money in the world.*

G is still drinking. He has been in trouble with the police since he has lived at this mother's home. Now I understand that it wasn't my fault. It was easy to blame myself, because the drinking did get worse over time, so it seemed to be because of me. But it wasn't. This is just the nature of addiction. It gets worse over time. It sneaks up on the addict and on those who live with him/her. It's like riding a bike up a hill – as the hill gradually gets harder to climb, you change gears on your bike to accommodate the steeper gradient and for a while, it seems manageable. But eventually, you run out of gears and you just have to get off the bike and walk away. It's not your fault that that you can't get up the hill, it's not that the bike isn't well made, it's just that the hill got too steep to climb.
I'm still fighting him legally and there's a chance that I'll get to keep my home, but I don't know. All I know is that I'm happier, stronger and that I'll be OK. I'll be just fine.

Two months later

A settlement conference was scheduled for March 2nd. Neither my lawyer nor I expected G to settle. I questioned the value of such a conference, but was told that it is a mandatory part of the process which precedes a hearing, and hopefully negates the necessity for one.

I have never felt so anxious. I would be confronted with two things I find very stressful: confrontation and G himself. His lawyer demanded half of everything on his client's behalf, and intimated that G could be entitled to even more. G had been drinking, I could tell. He wasn't shaking, and was very relaxed and confident, even smug. He had a bottle of what appeared to be water with him, but was instructed by his lawyer to drink the water supplied by the court which stood in a carafe with glasses on the conference table. The judge acted as facilitator, rather than decision maker, clarifying points of law and maintaining control of the proceedings. Amounts of money for the purposes of a pay out were traded back and forth, I conferred with my lawyer, he with his. More haggling ensued. The judge left the room, unimpressed with the "horse-trading". The amounts began to favor me more and more, and then it was over. He had settled. I was to pay him one lump sum, and then he would disappear from my life. I exited the doors of the court and felt reborn. I had lost money but regained my self-respect and dignity. And I kept my house. My father has helped me as much as he is able, and I have the continued support of my friends. I'm pretty broke, but I'm rich.

For the longest time, I could spy only the smallest glimmer of light at the end of this long, dark tunnel. But I'm through and although the light is still very bright, I'm getting used to it. I'm free."

—

Alcohol addiction is destructive for both the drinker and the people close to them. Different treatment must be forthcoming if we are to stop this avalanche of destruction.

In an Ideal World

The trouble is that none of these things are looked at in the beginning because no one really knows where the beginning was. And by the time the alcohol has caused enough trouble to get seen by medical staff, those staff are only treating the symptoms that present to them at the time. The symptoms the alcohol has caused - not the original cause.

In an ideal world those who are heading towards a future controlled by alcohol would be interrupted in their quest and given data that proved to them what damage they are doing. A truthful base to listen to or to leave. Ideal worlds are thin on the ground and we all know this is not about to happen. The young drinker of today knows that all those bad things will never happen to him. He can stop way before that happens. He is safe in this knowledge. That sort of thing only happens to old people anyway and he will not be old for ages. Why worry now?

Little does he know.

Education and Attitude

Education and a change in attitude can be the only key. Provide them with information early. Education that they are not diseased for life and what is causing them to be like they are.

The goal is to interrupt the addiction cycle earlier rather than later, before chaos and destruction have become the norm. Many, many people are sensible drinkers and will come to no harm. The budding alcoholic is a different animal entirely. This education is for those who are starting to wander aimlessly down the wrong road. The apprentice alcoholics of today. The hard core alcoholics of tomorrow. They may take no notice, although hopefully sometime in the future their brain will remember a few words of what they have learnt. It might save their life.

Attitudes on both sides of the fence need to change. We are achieving this in regards to cigarette smoking so why not in the area of harmful drinking?

The public's attitude has changed dramatically over the last decade in regards to cigarette smoking. Not so long ago smoking was everywhere. In theaters, in offices, in clubs and bars, in every public place. Every movie star was either lighting a cigarette or engulfed in a smoky haze. In a relatively short period of time this has changed and many people have become nonsmokers. Quit-lines use empowering language to encourage smokers to quit. A positive approach to quitting is the norm and no 12 step programs are mentioned.

The attitude that is held around heavy drinking/alcoholism needs to change as well. The general consensus is that these people are somehow flawed. They are not like us. They can stop drinking whenever they want to. They just don't really want to or they would have done it before now. There's not a lot that can be done for them. It's just how they are. If they went to AA and it didn't work they obviously didn't try hard enough. They didn't really want to stop. The general public thinks this way.
The drinker's attitude is that he was born with a rotten disease and will always be the same. He has to struggle with it all his life. Struggle through every day.

—

Attitudes must change. This will only happen when effective treatment is seen to be working. The news of effective help will spread. In books, on the internet and by word of mouth. Families of the alcoholic will tell others how their loved one has become well. At present when the problem is not directly affecting your own family you too may have the same opinions and attitude as above.

People do not want to be confronted with alcoholism in any way. They don't talk about it. The families are often ashamed. Once again harking back to the belief of their loved one being flawed. They would rather have them shut away and become someone else's problem.
I too have felt that way when life became too hard. Confronted with the horrors that play out, you wish someone else would take them away and deal with them. There is great relief when they are hospitalized. The guilt is huge but it is still a relief. They soon get discharged and life goes on.

The publicity given to celebrities and alcohol rehabilitation does nothing to enhance the image the public have. It seems as if these select few are admitted to an expensive treatment center, given treatment and discharged relatively quickly as being 'fixed.' This misconception is very often not true. Going in and out of rehab is portrayed as a short vacation done on a whim. The assumption here also is that only rich people can get helped because they can afford it. Yes attitudes need to change and will only do so with effective treatment.

The Wrong Diagnosis

As stated in 'Under the Influence' 80% or more of alcoholic patients could make lasting high quality recoveries. Sadly the psychological problems are 'treated' rather than the physical problems. Many professional people try to treat the psychological (of the mind) problems as the main cause of the addiction and continually ignore the physical (of the body) malnutrition, the body's reaction to toxins and hypoglycemia. The anxiety and depression which at present are diagnosed as the main problems when it is the physical problems that have led to the depression and anxiety.

In the early stages of alcoholism we do not see the physical deterioration of the body that the continued drinking has caused. But this is self-evident later on. If those trying to help them could see this physical decline earlier, today's treatment for alcoholics would be very different. It would be very obvious that the malnutrition of brain and body needs to be repaired and not merely try to talk the problem away.

Kevin always said that nothing in his early life, or later, could account for his drinking. He was often at a loss during counseling sessions to answer their questions. No amount of searching, other than to unearth a father, who also drank, could be found. Then this fact was seen as the cause and he was told to learn from the past and to stop drinking. Never was it mentioned that alcohol was changing his brain cells and making him behave irrationally. Never was nutrition mentioned to repair the damage. More depression and a truck load of futility are dumped on the alcoholic as he now begins to believe that he is mentally deficient because all the professionals are saying it is so. So he sinks deeper into despair, confirming to himself that he is a failure. He believes now that he really is worthless, which intensifies his shame and guilt. The more depressed and sure that he truly is mentally inept, the more he drinks. And is told he needs more psychological treatment. More talk therapy.

Many alcoholics hold responsible positions in the community, are highly paid and intelligent people. They are doubly confused as to what is happening to them. They cannot figure out why their brain is letting them down and understandably become worried, anxious, agitated and afraid.
Since alcohol is the only thing in the world that makes them feel better they turn once again to it, unknowingly adding to the damage already rampant in the body and brain.

The care the alcoholic needs is to be able to safely abstain from the alcohol that is poisoning him and be treated for the physical (of the body) problems that have been caused. Cravings will disappear when health is returned. For some this will be the first time in many many years they have felt anywhere near well. It will then be self-evident to the alcoholic that the psychological (of the mind) problems are indeed the result of the alcohol that has been consumed. He will see the altered brain causes him to present with abnormal behavior. Time must go into repair and recuperation or it will all be for nothing. It will be for the alcoholic alone to forge this new path into wellness. All we can do is present the facts that a continued personal nutritional plan with abstinence from alcohol must be adhered to for a healthy life. Just as a diabetic or any one allergic to a particular food must watch their diet so must the alcoholic. In years to come being an alcoholic should have as much relevance as having an allergy to dairy products. The cravings, the depression, the anxiety and stress will be disappear with the proper regime of biochemical repair.

The alcoholic will not be able to drink again, but it must be a personal choice to take the path towards health. They cannot be doing it for the family, for the partner, for the employer. It is their life to live as they see fit. We can offer the tools to enable that life to happen with work on their part. They must choose whether to take up those tools and become well as others have proved is possible.

Too Late

At present there isn't even an ambulance at the bottom of the cliff. In most cases it is an undertaker's vehicle.

For those who are not helped by an AA/12step program the only alternatives for a long time have been to become sober by themselves or to die slowly and painfully. The nutritional help is not new and has been available for some time. The success rates are good but seem to be seen by some as very 'new age'.

'If it is that good there must be something wrong with it' mentality. How strange. If some treatment places are achieving excellent results why not try their ways? We now have medical proof as to what is happening to their brains and why. Intensive nutritional treatment needs to be focused on bringing the brain and body back to health while simultaneously providing good counseling. Good outpatient facilities are a must. The cause has to be located whether it be physical or psychological or both, otherwise the addiction will continue in one form or another. If the alcoholic is dried out and discharged without nutritional repair and education he will head for the nearest liquor store and off he will go again. If the drinking does stop, there is the likelihood of another addiction occurring. This will arrive in the form gambling, compulsive shopping and hoarding. And the drinking will return.

We are really missing the boat as far as getting good nutritional education and treatment for these people early enough. Keeping on sending them to a 12 step program will not address these issues. The 88% who are not helped by this method are then left to wander in the wilderness. To become sober by themselves or not.

Over time they become so sick that it is very difficult to pull them back to health. All ambition has gone. All hope is lost. It is easier to give up, drink more and die slowly with every drink. I have seen it happen.

'It is the saddest of all things, when a person gives up'
Confucius 2500 years ago

Kevin

Perhaps we won't always succeed in helping these drinkers back to a healthy path. But we can try. We must offer all the options we know. We can then say we have done all we could with the knowledge available to us today.

Although sometimes it is just too hard to live with. Just too dam hard to get through each day. We then have to make choices ourselves. What is best for us? Those of us who live with the alcoholic. Because we have lives too.

Life is made up of choices and as explained fully in my first book we alone have to decide what we need to do. To stay with the alcoholic or not. It is not a simple choice, but one we need to make.

Not long after Kevin's death someone asked me if I missed him. The answer was 'I miss the person he used to be, not the person he had become.'

We continue to remember the good times. We cannot dwell on the bad.

He may not have appreciated being written about but if someone is helped he would not have minded. In the hope that we can continue to learn, to grow and to offer alternative methods towards a life free from addiction I will close with Kevin's own words from the end of a graduation speech after a residential stay.

"And finally to some of the more important tricks this old dog has learnt.
Be honest, both internally and externally, set clear boundaries, say no when appropriate and think through any problems rather than ignore or rush into them.

I wish each of you well in whatever journey you are taking and I hope you safely reach your chosen destination."

Websites and Books that combine new skills, empowerment and a fresh approach.

Those of us who live with an alcoholic partner day in and day out are too exhausted to be finding good books on how we can help them. We cannot spend hours trawling through websites looking for alternative help. It is difficult enough to get through each day. If the drinker is beginning to lose hope it is doubly difficult because depression also has to be contended with.

I have provided here a list of books and websites.

They are all alternatives to traditional AA/12 step programs. Proven choices are offered to naturally heal the damage that has been done to the brain and body. **Seven Weeks to Sobriety** and **Under the Influence** are must reads.

Seven Weeks to Sobriety by Dr Joan Mathews-Larson PhD with Keith W. Sehnert MD. <u>www.healthrecovery.com</u>
A must read for any alcoholic or for those living with them.
All nutrient and maintenance formulas are detailed in the book.

Under the Influence by James Robert Milam and Katherine Ketcham
Ten of millions Americans suffer from alcoholism, yet most people still wrongly believe that alcoholism is a psychological or moral problem, and that it can be cured by psychotherapy or sheer will power. Based on groundbreaking scientific research, *Under the Influence* examines the physical factors that set alcoholics and non-alcoholics apart, and suggests a bold, stigma-free way of understanding and treating the alcoholic.
How to tell if someone you know is an alcoholic. The progressive stages of alcoholism. How to get an alcoholic

into treatment -- and how to choose a treatment program. Why frequently prescribed drugs can be dangerous -- even fatal -- for alcoholics. How to ensure a lasting recovery.

Sober and Staying That Way: The Missing Link in the Cure for Alcoholism by Susan Powter
For almost forty years it has been known that alcoholism is a biochemical disease. In extreme exasperation, Powter asks the question, "Why have we just accepted the fact that there is no cure for alcoholism and that the only treatment available is through organizations like AA? Disease talk doesn't cure."

End Your Addiction Now – the Proven Nutritional Supplement Program that can set you Free by Dr Charles Gant and Greg Lewis PhD.
Dr Gant has successfully used a nutritional supplements approach to treat brain imbalance. He recommends a diet high in protein, brain-healthy fats, high fiber carbohydrates and supplements that include minerals, vitamins, and amino acids to heal the brain.   www.charlesgantmd.com

How to Defeat Alcoholism: Nutritional Guidelines for Getting Sober by Joseph Beasley. He states that diet and nutrition should be part of any alcoholic treatment program.

The Alcoholism and Addiction Cure – A Holistic Approach to Total Recovery by Chris Prentis.
www.passagesmalibu.com
A father's true story about helping his son and now many other people are staying sober the same way. A proven comprehensive holistic approach towards an effective recovery.

Handbook of Alcoholism Treatment Approaches: Effective Alternatives by Reid K Hester and William R Miller.

The Anatomy of Addiction: Why 12 Steps are Rarely the Answer by Drs Morteza and Karen Khaleghi who are addiction specialists and the founders of Creative Care in California.

AA – Not the Only Way by Melanie Solomon
www.aanottheonlyway.com   Melanie's story is mentioned earlier in this book.

www.alternatives-for-alcoholism.com Cynthia Perkins is a trained health professional and has had 20 years of uninterrupted sobriety. She has not attended an AA meeting in 17 years. She is of the opinion that the more educated you are about alcoholism the better chance you have of overcoming it. Different people respond to different treatments in different ways.

www.cassmd.com
Dr Hyla Cass a professor at UCLA School of medicine also uses a holistic approach.

www.holistichelp.net/alcoholism
Alcoholism is a very complex problem that is rampant in our society and had many variables that need to be addressed simultaneously. The success rate with mainstream treatment is poor at best. The nutrition and diet components are rarely addressed and most people are unaware of their extreme significance. Or that an alternative alcohol treatment exists.

www.drlwilson.com/Articles/alcoholism.htm

Quotes and Sayings I like

None of us can change our yesterdays,
But all of us can change our tomorrows - Colin Powell

The phrase "I can't" is the most powerful force of negation in the human psyche – Paul Scheele

Everything you want is just outside your comfort zone – Robert Allen

The significant problems we face cannot be solved by the same level of thinking that created them – Albert Einstein

You are the average of the five people you spend the most time with – Jim Rohn

Confidence is contagious. So is lack of confidence. – Vince Lombardi

Resentment is like drinking poison and then hoping it will kill your enemies – Nelson Mandela

You can be whatever type of person you choose to be. Your habits, your behaviors, your responses are all your choices.

When in doubt, tell the truth – Mark Twain

Make every stumbling block a stepping stone.

To make the right choices in life, you have to get in touch with your soul. To do this you need to experience solitude, which most people are afraid of, because in the silence you hear the truth and know the solutions -Deepak Chopra

In the long run we shape our lives, and we shape ourselves. The process never ends until we die. And the choices we make are ultimately our own responsibility.

Eleanor Roosevelt

Life is the sum of all our choices - Albert Camus

Each morning when I open my eyes I say to myself: I, not events, have the power to make me happy or unhappy today. I can choose which it shall be. Yesterday is dead, tomorrow hasn't arrived yet. I have just one day, today and I'm going to be happy in it – Groucho Marx

This above all to thine own self be true. - Shakespeare

Things don't change – we change - H Thoreau

Be who you are and say what you feel
Because those that matter don't mind
And those that mind don't matter - Theodor Seuss Geisel [Dr Seuss]

One evening a Cherokee elder told his grandson about the battle that goes on inside people. He said "My son, the battle is between the two "wolves" that live inside us all. One is Unhappiness. It is fear, worry, anger, jealousy, sorrow, self-pity, resentment and inferiority.
The other is Happiness. It is joy, love, serenity, kindness, generosity, truth, and compassion.
The grandson thought about this for a minute and then asked his grandfather "Which wolf wins?"
The old Cherokee simply replied, "The one you feed".

The Apprentice Alcoholic

Being completely unaware of what is happening in their body the apprentice alcoholic will obliviously forge ahead with their lives, drinking more than most. We are failing the young 'would-be alcoholic' of tomorrow by not making available truthful information regarding alcoholism.

A young drinker who may have a slight inkling that he has a problem is understandably reluctant to attend a meeting of usually older alcoholics and declare himself to be one of them. And nor should he have to. Perhaps he has not got that far, but where does he look for help?

Truthful education at an early age will do little to stop the budding alcoholic, although some way down the track he might remember what he was told some years before. If at least he can realize that he is not one of the lowest forms of life. He does not have a disease that he will never feel better from. And he does not have to battle through life struggling with each day.

Until the public perception, as well as that of the budding alcoholic, changes as to how alcoholism is to be treated, no progress will be made. We are failing them if we leave them to grow older without good help, if they want it.
The invisible progression of alcoholism will continue in their brain and body. We cannot leave it until many years later, when a lot of damage has been done and they begin to present with medical problems.
Perhaps they do not want to know, but the least we can do is offer truthful medical and scientific facts and not wishful thinking and faith.

81

INDEX

Please note:
The author is not a counselor, doctor, therapist, psychologist, psychiatrist, life coach or health professional. This book is my own personal opinion gleaned from living with an alcoholic partner, my husband.

It is not the intention of the author to provide any type of counseling in this book.

The opinions offered and thoughts conveyed, are those of the author.

No responsibility or liability can be accepted by the author for any actions taken by any person or organization.

If you fear for your own safety seek a safe refuge.

In an emergency the front of the phone book lists numbers for urgent help.

49617382R00048

Made in the USA
Columbia, SC
24 January 2019